Pope John XXIII

$\mathcal{P}$OPE $\mathcal{J}$OHN XXIII

$\mathcal{I}$N $\mathcal{M}$Y $\mathcal{O}$WN $\mathcal{W}$ORDS

Compiled and edited by
Anthony F. Chiffolo

Liguori
LIGUORI, MISSOURI

Published by Liguori Publications
Liguori, Missouri
http://www.liguori.org

Compilation copyright
1999 by Anthony F. Chiffolo

Library of Congress Cataloging-in-Publication Data

John XXIII, Pope, 1881–1963.
   In my own words / Pope John XXIII ; compiled and edited by
Anthony F. Chiffolo.
      p.   cm.
   ISBN 0-7648-0498-7
   1. John XXIII, Pope, 1881–1963 Quotations. I. Chiffolo,
Anthony F., 1959– . II. Title
   BX1378.2.A25 1999
   282'.092—dc21   99-26792
   [B]

The editor and publisher gratefully acknowledge permission to
reprint/reproduce copyrighted works granted by the publishers/
sources listed on page 112.

Printed in the United States of America
99 00 01 02 03   5 4 3 2 1
First Edition

May Jesus, Mary, and Joseph,

our joy and love,

be always with us

for our protection and happiness, and

for the protection and happiness

of our dear ones.

———

LETTER TO HIS NIECE AURELIA, JULY 30, 1952

CONTENTS

INTRODUCTION	IX
MY OWN LIFE	1
HUMILITY AND POVERTY	17
SUFFERING	25
GOD'S WILL AND DIVINE PROVIDENCE	31
HOLINESS	41
THE CHRISTIAN LIFE	55
JUSTICE AND CHARITY	63
PEACE	71
TRUTH	77
MODERN ISSUES	83
THE CHURCH AND THE SACRAMENTS	93
VATICAN II	105
PERMISSIONS AND ACKNOWLEDGMENTS	112

$\mathcal{I}$NTRODUCTION

It is difficult to imagine that anyone living in the last decades of the twentieth century can have escaped the influence of Pope John XXIII. So many people have been personally moved by his warmth, sincerity, and personal holiness that he has come to be known as the Good Pope. Others, impressed with his ability to influence global political events during a crucial period in world history, call him the Pope of Peace. Still others, having found comfort and sound advice in his pastoral words, refer to him as the Parish Priest of the World or, simply, as the Great Priest. Many more millions around the globe, both within and beyond the boundaries of Roman Catholicism, hail him as Everyone's Pope for his boldness in opening the windows of a musty Church and convening an ecumenical council that was truly inclusive and global in scope. *Time* magazine saluted him as Man of the Year for 1962; history may well show him to be the most consequential person of the century.

But if appearances and circumstances were determinative, Angelo Giuseppe Roncalli would have lived an obscure life and then entered unnoticed onto the list of the faithful departed. Born on November 25, 1881, in the village of Sotto il Monte, outside Bergamo, in the hills of northern Italy, Angelo was the first son after three daughters of Giovanni and Marianna Roncalli. They were eventually to have nine children, scratching a living off the land as poor tenant farmers. Though sensing an early calling to the priesthood, as an average student with no family fortune to back his clerical career, Roncalli did not seem destined to be anything more than a faithful, hard-working parish priest ministering diligently to other poor farmers. Indeed, poverty was a hallmark of his entire life, as was his love and concern for his large and often turbulent family.

Apparently, God had other things in store for this anonymous yet remarkable soul. From the time he entered the minor seminary in Bergamo at the age of eleven, Roncalli exhibited an unmistakable call to personal holiness. Concerned with overcoming what he considered excessive pride and self-love, he progressed rapidly in his formation and was called to the Apollinare, the Pontifical Roman Seminary, in 1901, where he quickly distinguished himself and earned the prize in Hebrew language studies. Though military duty interrupted his studies in 1901–02, he was ordained deacon the following year and priest on August 10, 1904.

Yet after his ordination he returned to his origins, serving as secretary to Bishop Giacomo Radini Tedeschi in Bergamo. Roncalli was a hard worker, and during his service to the bishop he also taught Church history in the diocesan seminary, started a small diocesan newsletter, *La Vita Diocesana*, and served as secretary for the diocesan synod. In 1915 he was recalled to military service, first as a sergeant in the medical corps and then as a chaplain in the military hospital. He served until the end of World War I, when he became spiritual director of the Bergamo seminary.

In 1921 Pope Benedict XV summoned Roncalli to Rome, tasking him with the reorganization of the Society for the Propagation of the Faith. That accomplished, Pope Pius XI assigned Roncalli as Apostolic Visitor to Bulgaria in 1925, giving him the title archbishop of Areopolis. Bulgaria's first papal envoy in more than six hundred years, he was sent to minister to the scant fifty thousand Roman Catholics in this out-of-the-way country suspicious of Rome and committed to the Eastern Orthodox Church. It seems that he was again given an out-of-the-way assignment, though he was promoted to Apostolic Delegate in 1931.

Because of his success under difficult circumstances in Bulgaria, Pope Pius XII promoted Roncalli to Apostolic Administrator of the Apostolic Vicariate of Istanbul—a more prestigious post than Bulgaria, though one with even fewer Catholics and more problems—in 1934, with the title archbishop of Mesembria. In 1939 the pope expanded his area of responsibility, assigning him as Apostolic Delegate to Turkey and Greece, as the world was exploding into war.

After the war, impressed with the course Roncalli had steered through the diplomatic shoals of Turkish and Greek relations, Pope Pius XII plucked Roncalli from Southeastern Europe and sent him to France as Apostolic Nuncio, the Vatican's most eminent diplomatic post. His job was to help heal the wartime wounds of one of Europe's most historically Catholic nations, and his wit, practical wisdom, invincible faith, and never-failing optimism— as well as his love of good cooking—inspired French Catholics and non-Catholics alike to rapprochement. His service in Paris helped restore peace among a people fractured by history.

In 1953 the pope called Roncalli back to Italy, making him cardinal and Patriarch of Venice. His mildness and tranquillity won over the Venetians, though he convened a diocesan synod in 1957 and continued to upset the conservative Vatican curia by making distinctions between atheistic Communism and ideal Socialism. When the pope died in 1958, Roncalli was called to Rome for the conclave.

To the world's great surprise, Roncalli was elected pope on October 28, 1958, and he took the name John after his models in religious life: John the Baptist, the prophet of Christ, and John the Beloved, the disciple of Love. And he immediately changed the face of the papacy as he became at once bishop of Rome in the truest sense, refusing to sequester himself behind the Vatican's walls but rather daring to visit churches, hospitals, even prisons to minister to his flock.

Pope John XXIII also quickly became an outspoken spokesman for peace. He reigned at a particularly dangerous time as superpower confronted superpower in a nuclear face-off, and his exhortations and appeals did much to prevent a third world war. For his efforts he was awarded the International Peace Prize of the Eugenio Balzan Foundation, and his encyclical on peace, *Pacem in Terris* (1963), is still hailed as a milestone in the effort to secure peace among nations.

His other great encyclical, *Mater et Magistra* (1961), continues to arouse controversy as the Church and its members consider their proper role in the modern world. In all, he penned eight encyclicals and various letters and exhortations whose influence has extended well beyond the borders of Roman Catholicism.

But Pope John XXIII will be remembered most for convening the Second Vatican Council. Elected at an advanced age, he was expected to serve only as a short-term, status-quo pope, but he again surprised the world—and particularly the curia—by calling for an ecumenical council, to be convened in the Vatican. His purpose—to open the windows and air out the Church—excited many Catholics and non-Catholics alike and frightened some others, both within and without the Church, but in 1962 he convened the council that would change the face of Roman Catholicism in the twentieth century and beyond, making it once again the Church of believers and nonbelievers alike. Certainly the changes in the practice of Christianity that he set in motion, as well as the atmosphere of open dialogue that he supported, will continue to renew the Church in unforeseen ways.

Pope John XXIII was not to see the conclusion of the council he convened, for he was sick with cancer during its opening session, and he died on June 3, 1963, before the bishops were scheduled to reconvene. Yet though he reigned as pope for only a short five years, history already considers him one of the greatest popes. In his holy example of abandoning himself to the Divine Will, he showed people how to live, and his words—as the selections in this collection demonstrate—continue to be a source of profound inspiration. As future generations of Christians take these words to heart and seek to live out the spirit of Vatican II, people across the globe will find their lives indelibly enriched by the bountiful spirit of the Good Pope.

– A F C

$\mathcal{M}$Y OWN LIFE

*O Lord, listen to this blind man
who calls out to you as you pass by,
and implores you to help him,
you who are indeed the light of my eyes!
Give me light that I may see:
"Lord, that I may see!"*

JOURNAL OF A SOUL, FEBRUARY, 1900

$\mathcal{W}$e are where we usually are: I desire nothing more nor less than what the Lord continues to give me. I thank him and I bless him every day: ready for anything.

RETREAT NOTES, ADVENT, 1961

$\mathcal{I}$ have found that the Lord always helps me, provided that I strip myself of all selfish desires and am willing to renounce everything for his sake.

LETTER TO HIS NIECE ENRICA, JANUARY 3, 1942

$\mathcal{I}$ live by the sun, from day to day. But the sun is faithful. Every now and then it seems to hide, but it soon comes back more glorious than ever.

LETTER TO HIS BROTHER GIOVANNI,
JANUARY 15, 1954

The Lord has given me much happiness in my life, because for a long time now I have accustomed myself not to take much notice of the failings of other people, but to think that I too have my own faults. I have learned to keep silent, to forgive at once and from my heart, to do good to those who ill-treat me, and above all to follow humbly the road that Providence has opened up before me, content to live each day as it comes and keeping constantly in my mind the thought of death and of paradise.

LETTER TO HIS NIECE ENRICA, AUGUST 8, 1945

I remember that when I was a child I used to implore the Lord most fervently to make the old Roncallis talk to each other a little. And I used to wonder: how will they ever get to heaven if the Lord says we must all love each other and trust each other with brotherly charity?

LETTER TO HIS BROTHER GIOVANNI,
CHRISTMAS, 1948

$\mathscr{I}$ am ready for any event, and I try to do every day what the Lord wants from me, day by day, with no care for tomorrow and without making many plans. I do all I can hour by hour, with great confidence and trust, and I see that in this way one can go far and receive many blessings.

LETTER TO HIS BROTHER GIOVANNI, APRIL 5, 1956

$\mathscr{W}$ ho am I? Where do I come from? Where am I going? I am nothing. Everything I possess, my being, life, understanding, will and memory—all were given me by God, so all belong to him. Twenty short years ago all that I see around me was already here; the same sun, moon and stars, the same mountains, seas, deserts, beasts, plants and men; everything was proceeding in its appointed way under the watchful eyes of Divine Providence. And I? I was not here. Everything was being done without me, nobody was thinking of me, nobody could imagine me, even in dreams, because I did not exist.

And you, O God, with a wonderful gesture of love, you who are from the beginning and before all time, you drew me forth from my nothingness, you gave me being, life, a soul, in fact all the faculties of my body and spirit; you opened my eyes to this light which sheds its radiance around me, you created me. So you are my Master and I am your creature. I am nothing without you, and through you I am all that I am. I can do nothing without you; indeed, if at every moment you did not support me I should slip back whence I came, into nothingness. This is what I am. And yet I am boastful and display with pride before the eyes of God all the blessings he has showered on me, as if they were my own. Oh what a fool I am!

JOURNAL OF A SOUL, FEBRUARY, 1900

The older I grow the more I find that supreme wisdom, the only true wisdom, is still found more in the little, simple books which are closest to the Gospel, than in the great treatises which attract our curiosity.

LETTER TO HIS NEPHEW BATTISTA, FEBRUARY 24, 1950

$\mathscr{A}$s I draw near to my seventieth year I see in the clearest light—an anticipation of the light of heaven—the fundamental importance of the command to be charitable *in thought, word, and deed.*

LETTER TO HIS NEPHEW BATTISTA, MARCH 14, 1948

$\mathscr{I}$ keep myself ready and prepared for death every day, and for a good death, desiring nothing else but the Lord's will....living in this way, every day being ready and prepared for a good death, ends by filling my heart with a profound and serene sense of peace, even greater than I had before, surely a foretaste of heaven where our dear ones are awaiting us.

LETTER TO HIS SISTER MARIA, JANUARY 8, 1955

$\mathscr{M}$y personal tranquillity, which makes so great an impression on the world, consists completely in this: to persevere in obedience as I always have, and not to desire or pray to live longer, not even for one day beyond the time when the angel of death will come to call me and take me to paradise, as I am confident he will.

LETTER TO HIS BROTHER SAVERIO, DECEMBER 3, 1961

$\mathcal{I}$ am like a picture which, although cleansed of those stains which made it unrecognizable, is still covered with a layer of specks of dust which, as it were, casts a shade over the whole painting and makes it displeasing to the eye. I am in exactly the same state as these neglected old pictures. So why should I be surprised if I do not feel within me the constant workings of grace and the fire of love, when these little negligences of mine stand in the way?

So I must do as we do with these pictures, when we want to restore them and make them look as beautiful as when they left the painter's hand. A good cleansing with oil is what they need, to make them recognizable. Yes, I must make a clean sweep of all these imperfections.

JOURNAL OF A SOUL, NOVEMBER 20, 1898

$\mathcal{N}$ot one drop of blood of Jesus can avail the rebel angels, yet theirs was merely a sin of thought, and their first at that. For me, who sin so frequently, all the fruits of the Passion are available, not once but time and time again. And still I keep my God waiting for me! What a miracle of mercy! and how shameful for me!

JOURNAL OF A SOUL, ADVENT, 1902

$\mathcal{H}$ail, Christ the King! You summon me to fight your battles and, without a moment's delay, with all the enthusiasm of my twenty years and the grace you have given me, I boldly enlist in the ranks of your volunteers. I dedicate myself to your service, for life or death. You offer me your Cross for a standard and a weapon. I place my right hand on this invincible weapon and give you my solemn word, swearing with all the fervor of my youthful heart absolute fidelity until death. So I, whom you created your servant, have become your soldier, I put on your uniform, I gird on your sword, I am proud to call myself a knight of Christ. Give me a soldier's heart, a knight's valor, O Jesus, and I will always be by your side in the rough moments of life, in sacrifices, in ordeals, in battles—and still with you in the hour of victory. And since the signal for the fight has not yet sounded for me, while I remain in my tent, waiting for my hour to strike, you must teach me by your shining example how to try out my valor against my own interior enemies, so as to get rid of these first. They are so many, O Jesus, and they are without mercy! There is one especially who is up to every trick; he is proud and cunning, he clings to me, he pretends to want to make peace and then he makes fun of me, he offers terms, he even follows me into my good deeds.

Lord Jesus, you know who that is: my self-love, the spirit of pride, presumption, and vanity. Help me to get rid of him once and for all or, if that is not possible, at least to hold him in subjection so that, unhampered in my movements, I may run to the breach, stand among the warriors who defend your holy cause, and sing with you the hymn of salvation.

JOURNAL OF A SOUL, ADVENT, 1902

*A*bove all, I am grateful to the Lord for the temperment he has given me, which preserves me from anxieties and tiresome perplexities. I feel I am under obedience in all things and I have noticed that this disposition, in great things and in small, gives me, unworthy as I am, a strength of daring simplicity, so wholly evangelical in its nature that it demands and obtains universal respect and edifies many. "Lord, I am not worthy. O Lord, be always my strength and the joy of my heart. My God, my mercy."

JOURNAL OF A SOUL, ADVENT, 1959

$\mathcal{I}$ love to think of how Jesus founded his Church! Instead of summoning the wise and the learned from the academies, the synagogues, and the schools, he cast his loving eyes on twelve poor fishermen, rough, ignorant men. He admitted them to his school, shared with them his most secret thoughts, made them the object of his most loving care, and entrusted to them the great mission of transforming mankind.

In the fullness of time Jesus has been pleased to call me also to extend his kingdom and to have some share in the work of the apostles. He took me, a country lad, from my home, and with the affection of a loving mother he has given me all I needed. I had nothing to eat and he provided food for me, I had nothing to wear and he clothed me, I had no books to study and he provided those also. At times I forgot him and he always gently recalled me. If my affection for him cooled, he warmed me in his breast, at the flame with which his Heart is always burning. His enemies and the enemies of his Church surrounded me, set snares for me, dragged me out into the midst of the world, into the mire and filth, and yet he has preserved me from all ill, he has not allowed the sea to swallow me up....and he still cares for me without respite, day and night, more than a mother cares for her child. Yet after all this, in return for so much tenderness, he asks me anxiously one thing only: My son, do you love me? Lord, Lord, how can I answer you? See my tears, my throbbing heart, my trembling lips, and the pen that slips from my fingers…What can I say? "Lord, you know that I love you."

JOURNAL OF A SOUL, ADVENT, 1902

*T*he more mature I grow in years and experience the more I recognize that the surest way to make myself holy…lies in the constant effort to reduce everything, principles, aims, position, business, to the utmost simplicity and tranquillity; I must always take care to strip my vines of all useless foliage and spreading tendrils, and concentrate on what is truth, justice, and charity, above all charity. Any other way of behaving is nothing but affectation and self-assertion; it soon shows itself in its true colors and becomes a hindrance and a mockery.

JOURNAL OF A SOUL, NOVEMBER, 1948

O Jesus, here I am before you. You are suffering and dying for me, old as I am now and drawing near the end of my service and my life. Hold me closely, and near to your heart, letting mine beat with yours. I love to feel myself bound forever to you with a gold chain, woven of lovely, delicate links.

The first link: the justice which obliges me to find my God wherever I turn.

The second link: the providence and goodness which will guide my feet.

The third link: love for my neighbor, unwearying and most patient.

The fourth link: the sacrifice that must always be my lot, and that I will and must welcome at all times.

The fifth link: the glory that Jesus promises me in this life and in eternity.

JOURNAL OF A SOUL, AUGUST 14, 1961

*A*t the moment of death shall I be content or discontent with my life?

JOURNAL OF A SOUL, AUGUST 16, 1898

$\mathcal{I}$ ask pardon of those whom I have unwittingly offended, of all to whom I have not been a source of edification. I feel that I have nothing to forgive anyone, for all who have known and dealt with me—including those who have offended me, scorned me, held me in bad esteem (with good reason, for that matter), or have been a source of affliction to me—I regard solely as brothers and benefactors, to whom I am grateful and for whom I pray and always will pray.

SPIRITUAL TESTAMENT AND LAST WISHES

$\mathcal{W}$hat did I feel upon learning that I had been elected Pope? Much emotion, to be sure, and a host of anxieties. But also the same sensation as a baby in swaddling clothes, because the cassock which they had slipped over me was very tight and I felt as though I were wrapped up like a mummy.

WIT AND WISDOM OF GOOD POPE JOHN

$\mathcal{A}$ basic rule for the Pope's conduct is this one of always resting content with his *present* state, and not getting all tangled up with the *future*, but instead leaving it in the Lord's hands without making too many plans or merely human provisions, and being careful not to speak of it with any ease and assurance to anyone whatsoever.

RETREAT NOTES, AUGUST 12, 1961

$\mathcal{S}$ince the Lord chose me, unworthy as I am, for this great service, I feel I have no longer any special ties in this life, no family, no earthly country or nation, nor any particular preferences with regard to studies or projects, even good ones. Now, more than ever, I see myself only as the humble and unworthy "servant of God and servant of the servants of God." The whole world is my family. This sense of belonging to everyone must give character and vigor to my mind, my heart, and my actions.

JOURNAL OF A SOUL, ADVENT, 1959

$\mathcal{A}$s for the goal to be reached in my life, I must:

1) Desire only to be just and holy, and in this *way* to please God.
2) Direct everything, thoughts and actions, toward the growth, the service, the glory of Holy Church.
3) Feeling that I am called by God, and precisely for this, remain perfectly calm about all that happens not only with regard to me, but also with regard to the Church, while still laboring always in her behalf and suffering with Christ for her.
4) Remain always resigned to Divine Providence.
5) Recognize myself always in my nothingness.
6) Always plan my day with clear vision and perfect order.

RETREAT NOTES, AUGUST 14, 1961

$\mathcal{I}$ find that I am still at the very beginning of the journey which I have undertaken, and this makes me feel ashamed. I thought I could have been a saint by this time, and instead I am still as miserable as before.

All this must humiliate me profoundly and make me realize what a good-for-nothing I am. Humility, humility, still more humility! However, in all my distress I can still thank the Lord for not having abandoned me as I deserved. Thanks be to God, I still have the will to be good, and with this I must go on. Go on, do I say? I must start again from the beginning. Well, I will do so. What am I waiting for? "In the name of the Father and of the Son and of the Holy Ghost, under the protection of the Virgin Mary and blessed Joseph" let us go forward.

JOURNAL OF A SOUL, MARCH 20, 1898

HUMILITY AND POVERTY

All are worthy of esteem
who do their duty humbly at all times.

LETTER TO HIS NEPHEW SAVERIO,
AUGUST 14, 1950

*E*arthly honors count for nothing, and money and wealth count even less and are extremely dangerous, but holiness and the effort to make others holy is the height of human happiness; this is of the greatest importance for our present life and the life to come.

LETTER TO HIS FAMILY, JULY 30, 1944

*T*he Lord wants our good will, day by day, and the destruction of our self-love, for his sake. The rest is all in his hands.

LETTER TO HIS NIECE GIUSEPPINA,
SEPTEMBER 24, 1944

*O*nly a few hours more—and this year too will come to an end and pass into history. I too finish the year and await the new dawn with joy. How many more years shall I see before I too cast anchor in the harbor of eternity? Perhaps many, perhaps few, possibly not even one whole year.

My Lord Jesus, "your years will never come to an end, and you have numbered mine." In whatever year you may call me, may I be found with my lamp full of oil, lest you cast me out into the shadow of death.

Meanwhile I go down on my knees before my God and, recalling his kindnesses to me this year, I humble myself in the dust and thank him with all my heart.

JOURNAL OF A SOUL, DECEMBER 31, 1902

Certain words of the Gospel are the central point and precept which comprehends and embraces in itself all the others: "Learn from me, for I am meek and humble of heart" [Matthew 11:29]. This is the great principle of gentleness and humility.

CORONATION ADDRESS, NOVEMBER 4, 1958

What gives a man dignity is not his wealth or good fortune or noble birth but a worthy and virtuous life and the dignity of his labour.

LETTER TO HIS COUSIN AGNESE, MAY 4, 1946

$\mathscr{I}$ too am sometimes made uncomfortable by my poverty, but we must not complain. This humble acceptance of poverty draws down upon us the Lord's most precious graces. But this does not mean that we need not do our best to improve our material conditions. We should do this, but without falling into the sin of avarice, which hardens the heart. We must enjoy from day to day whatever the Lord sends us. We must prepare for tomorrow, like busy ants, but not die of hunger today in order to try to assure for ourselves an uncertain tomorrow.

LETTER TO HIS FAMILY, SEPTEMBER 26, 1948

$\mathscr{N}$ight has fallen; the clear, bright stars are sparkling in the cold air; noisy, strident voices rise to my ear from the city, voices of the revelers of this world who celebrate with their merrymaking the poverty of their Savior. Around me in their rooms my companions are asleep, and I am still wakeful, thinking of the mystery of Bethlehem.

Come, come Jesus, I await you.

Mary and Joseph, knowing the hour is near, are turned away by the townsfolk and go out into the fields to look for a shelter. I am a poor shepherd, I have only a wretched stable, a small manger, some wisps of straw. I offer all these to you, be pleased to come into my poor hovel. Make haste, O Jesus, I offer you my heart; my soul is poor and bare of virtues, the straws of so many imperfections will prick you and make you weep—but O my Lord what can you expect? this little is all I have. I am touched by your poverty, I am moved to tears, but I have nothing better to offer you. Jesus, honor my soul with your presence, adorn it with your graces. Burn this straw and change it into a soft couch for your most holy body.

Jesus, I am here waiting for your coming. Wicked men have driven you out and the wind is like ice. Come into my heart. I am a poor man but I will warm you as well as I can. At least be pleased that I wish to welcome you warmly, to love you dearly and sacrifice myself for you.

But in your own way you are rich and you see my needs. You are a flame of charity, and you will purge my heart of all that is not your own most holy Heart. You are uncreated holiness, and you will fill me with those graces which give new life to my soul. O Jesus, come, I have so much to tell you, so many sorrows to confide, so many desires, so many promises, so many hopes.

I want to adore you, to kiss you on the brow,
O tiny Jesus, to give myself to you once more,
forever. Come, my Jesus, delay no longer, come,
be my guest.

Alas! it is already late, I am overcome with
sleep and my pen slips from my fingers. Let me
sleep a little, O Jesus, while your Mother and
Saint Joseph are preparing the room.

I will lie down to rest here, in the fresh
night air. As soon as you come the splendor of
your light will dazzle my eyes. Your angels will
awaken me with sweet hymns of glory and
peace, and I shall run forward with joy to
welcome you and to offer you my own poor
gifts, my home, all the little I have. I will
worship you and show you all my love, with the
other shepherds who have joined me and with
the angels of heaven, singing hymns of glory to
your Sacred Heart. Come, I am longing for you.

JOURNAL OF A SOUL, DECEMBER 24, 1902

We may be poor, but poverty, humility, and
happiness are together better than wealth,
pride, ambition, and the pursuit of pleasure.

LETTER TO HIS FAMILY, DECEMBER 22, 1950

*W*hat honors our lives is not wealth or noble rank but the nobility of Christian principles, frankly professed with meekness and humility of heart, and the capacity to love the Cross and to consider all worldly things as a preparation for eternal life. The rest is worth nothing.

LETTER TO HIS NIECE ENRICA, AUGUST 6, 1952

*W*hat matters is that I should never be ashamed of my poverty, indeed I should be proud of it, just as the lords of this world are proud of their noble lineage, their titles of nobility, their liveries. I am of the same family as Christ—what more can I want? Do I need anything? Providence will abundantly provide, as always hitherto.

JOURNAL OF A SOUL, ADVENT, 1902

$\mathcal{H}$ave no fear for tomorrow: Providence will care for all. We must learn to live like poor people in order to acquire the love of poverty, but always trusting in God, day by day. You will see that you will never lack for anything. And in any case, all things, even suffering, will be turned to our greater good.

LETTER TO HIS SISTERS ANCILLA AND MARIA,
APRIL 27, 1944

SUFFERING

*Every one of us has his own service
to render—some serve by working
and some by suffering.
The reward of suffering is even more
generous and more certain.*

LETTER TO HIS BROTHER SAVERIO, APRIL 6, 1947

$\mathcal{M}$isfortunes are by no means rare events in families—and cause many tears to flow. But faith is here to show us that if God has permitted us to suffer, he will help us to endure.

DAILY PAPAL MESSAGES

$\mathcal{M}$any of us are inclined to think of all the physical sufferings of this world as evils, absolute evils. We have forgotten that pain is the legacy we have inherited from Adam; we have forgotten that the only real evil is sin, which offends the Lord, and that we must look to the Cross of Jesus as the apostles, martyrs, saints, teachers, and witnesses looked to it. For in the Cross we find strength and salvation, and in the love of Christ there is no life without suffering.

Thanks be to God, not all souls turn rebellious under the burden of pain. There are some infirm people who understand the meaning of suffering and are aware of the opportunities they have been given to contribute to the salvation of the world—and so they accept their life of pain as Jesus Christ accepted his, as most holy Mary accepted hers on the feast of her Purification, and as her chaste and faithful husband Saint Joseph accepted his.

What more useful counsel can we give than this: never let your gaze turn away from the Cross of Jesus, which the liturgy invites you to contemplate?

Look at this Cross, my beloved children, when you have to suffer. If those who are in pain make this their rule of life they will never feel alone; in paradise they will see the rich fruits of their spiritual efforts, in paradise where there are no more tears, or pain or separations, and no more possibility of offending God.

DAILY PAPAL MESSAGES

$\mathcal{T}$he scene in the garden strengthens and encourages us to force all our will to an acceptance, a full acceptance, of suffering sent or permitted by God: "Not my will but thine be done" (Luke 22:42). Words which tear the heart and heal it again, for they teach us what passionate fervor the Christian can and must feel if he is to suffer with Christ who suffers, and gives us the final certainty of the indescribable merits he obtained for us, the certainty of the divine life, a life which today is lived in grace and tomorrow in glory.

DAILY PAPAL MESSAGES

$\mathcal{W}$e must never feel saddened by the very straitened circumstances in which we live; we must be patient, look above and think of paradise.

Paradise, paradise! We shall find our rest there, do you understand? there we shall suffer no more; we shall receive the reward of our works and of our sufferings, if we have borne them with patience.

Direct all your actions and your sacrifices to this end: that they may all serve to make you more happy and content in paradise.

Think of what the good Jesus did and suffered for us. He endured great poverty, he worked from morning to night, was slandered, persecuted, and ill-treated in every way and crucified by the very people whom he loved so much.

We must learn from him not to complain, not to get angry, and not to lose our tempers with anyone, and not to nurse in our hearts any dislike for those we believe have injured us, but to have compassion for one another, because we all have our faults, some of one kind, some of another, and we must love everyone. You understand what I mean? Everyone, even those who injure, or have injured us; we must forgive, and pray for these too. Perhaps in God's eyes they are better than we are.

...this is the only way to live happily, even in this world, even in the midst of so many hardships.

LETTER TO HIS FAMILY, FEBRUARY 16, 1901

*T*he Lord's Passion and his Resurrection show us that there are two lives: one which we barely live, the other for which we long. Is not Jesus, who deigned to bear this poor earthly life for our sake, able to give us the life we desire? He wants us to believe this, to believe in his love for us, and in his eagerness to share with us his own riches, as once he chose to share our poverty. It was because we all have to die that he chose to die too.

We all know this already: our end and our beginning, birth and death. This is common knowledge and clear for all to see in our own sphere. Our sphere is this earth: the sphere of the angels is heaven. Our Lord came from one sphere to the other, from the realm of life to the realm of death; from the land of bliss to the land of toil and sorrow.

He came to bring us his gifts, and to bear with patience our sufferings—to bring us his gifts in secret, and publicly to bear our wretched lot, to show himself as a man and to conceal his divinity, to appear in the flesh, while the Divine Word was hidden from our eyes. The Word was hidden but it was not silent: it taught us to endure in patience.

WRITINGS AND ADDRESSES
WHILE PATRIARCH OF VENICE

GOD'S WILL AND DIVINE PROVIDENCE

Nothing done in God's will is done in vain on this earth.

DAILY PAPAL MESSAGES

$\mathcal{Y}$ou know that it is not the noise we make in our lives, or the things we see, that count, but the love with which we do the will of God.

DAILY PAPAL MESSAGES

$\mathcal{I}$ think that everything has gone well for me just because I have always tried to obey God's will and not my own. By doing this you will find everything will come right for you in the end, for yourself and for your dear ones.

LETTER TO HIS BROTHER SAVERIO, CHRISTMAS 1948

$\mathcal{W}$hen you feel that your longing for something is too keen and is causing you pain, then give up all thought of it and abandon yourselves effortlessly to the will of God. We are all like wayfarers in this world: some arrive early and some late. We often have to change our train or coach, or our traveling companions. We grieve over these partings, but the Lord blesses them and turns them to good account. What matters is that sooner or later we all arrive at our goal.

LETTER TO HIS SISTER ANCILLA, JANUARY 31, 1926

$\mathcal{W}$e must be like the stars in the sky; as the Lord calls them, one by one, they answer: here I am, ready. Once we have left the self behind, in our total consecration to God, we raise ourselves gradually until, certainly with an effort but fairly soon, we reach the perfect state of total dedication to the Lord's will. And this is a foretaste of heaven.

LETTER TO HIS NIECE ANNA, DECEMBER 14, 1946

$\mathcal{W}$e must know how to await with confidence whatever the Lord may send and never lose heart, even when we know that we are very weak and cannot go far along the road. Our road will be long or short as the Lord wills. But we shall follow it faithfully and with determination even if we break our legs over it…as Saint Joan once said of herself. The Lord blesses and strengthens a good will and crowns it with success.

LETTER TO HIS NIECE GIUSEPPINA, FEBRUARY 13, 1949

$\mathcal{L}$et us pray, let us pray always about everything, and may all be done according to the will of God, to his honor and glory.

Yes, "to the greater glory of God!" Amen.

JOURNAL OF A SOUL, SEPTEMBER 20, 1898

"$\mathcal{F}$riend, why are you here?" To know God, to love him and to serve him all my life, and after death to enjoy him forever in paradise. All the answers of the learned are not worth these few words from the children's catechism. The duties of my life are all contained in these three words. This is all I have to do: to know, love, and serve God, always and at all costs; God's will must be mine and I must seek it only, even in the slightest things.

JOURNAL OF A SOUL, APRIL, 1903

$\mathcal{W}$e must go on living from day to day, always ready to receive whatever the Lord sends.

LETTER TO HIS PARENTS, MAY 24, 1933

_H_ave courage and do not worry. Take each day as it comes, and do not tie your head up until it is broken.

LETTER TO HIS SISTERS ANCILLA AND MARIA,
OCTOBER 16, 1942

_Y_ou must live each day as it comes, and proceed arm in arm with Providence, not try to race ahead.

LETTER TO HIS NEPHEW BATTISTA, AUGUST 4, 1945

_E_very soul which presents itself to the Lord for the last judgment has reason to fear. But the Lord's mercy is infinitely greater than our human weakness and covers it all in his light and peace.

LETTER TO HIS NEPHEW BATTISTA,
DECEMBER 13, 1951

_W_e never pray to the Lord in vain, for he is always good and merciful to us poor mortals and especially to those most heavily burdened with his Cross.

LETTER TO HIS NEPHEW BATTISTA,
DECEMBER 13, 1951

$\mathscr{A}$s long as our will is firm, and the love of Jesus is in our hearts, with the desire to seek and follow the divine will in all things rather than our own, we must fear nothing, not even storms. Our sun is always shining, even when hidden from us by clouds.

LETTER TO HIS NIECE GIUSEPPINA, MAY 7, 1952

$\mathscr{W}$e must keep calm and live from day to day, leaving the Lord to do his own work; this is the surest way to succeed.

LETTER TO HIS NIECE MARIA, APRIL 10, 1955

$\mathscr{N}$ot a single day will be without its grace and salvation, and its joy.

LETTER TO HIS NIECE ENRICA, SEPTEMBER 3, 1955

$\mathcal{W}$e must recognize that wickedness is in us because, although the temptation comes from without, the grace to resist it is entirely at our disposal and is stronger than the temptation.

JOURNAL OF A SOUL, NOVEMBER 27, 1940

$\mathcal{I}$n a word, place yourself in the arms and near the Heart of Jesus in the Blessed Sacrament, and then leave all to him. He will form you, he will open your eyes: he will teach you all that you must do; he will make of you, you who are worth nothing, a real priest of his, full of love for him.

THE "LITTLE RULES" OF ASCETIC LIFE

$\mathcal{E}$very day is the right day for the lost sheep to return to the care of the tender shepherd who calls to it and goes out to seek it with great longing.

Any day, any week, a sinner may return to God.

WRITINGS AND ADDRESSES
WHILE PATRIARCH OF VENICE

Genesis relates how God gave two commandments to our first parents: to transmit human life—"Increase and multiply" [Genesis 1:28]—and to bring nature into their service—"Fill the earth and subdue it" [Genesis 1:28]. These two commandments are complementary.

Nothing is said in the second of these commandments about destroying nature. On the contrary, it must be brought into the service of human life.

We are sick at heart, therefore, when we observe the contradiction which has beguiled so much modern thinking. On the one hand we are shown the fearful specter of want and misery which threatens to extinguish human life, and on the other hand we find that scientific discoveries, technical inventions, and economic resources are being used to provide terrible instruments of ruin and death.

A provident God grants sufficient means to the human race to find a dignified solution to the problems attendant upon the transmission of human life. But these problems can become difficult of solution, or even insoluble, if man, led astray in mind and perverted in will, turns to such means as are opposed to right reason, and seeks ends that are contrary to his social nature and the intentions of Providence.

MATER ET MAGISTRA

*I*n this earthly life, when children have to make their way along a path beset with obstacles and snares, their fathers take care to call upon the help of those who can look after them and come to their aid in adversity. In the same way our Father in heaven has charged his angels to come to our assistance during our earthly journey which leads us to our blessed fatherland, so that, protected by the angels' help and care, we may avoid the snares upon our path, subdue our passions, and, under this angelic guidance, follow always the straight and sure road which leads to paradise.

DAILY PAPAL MESSAGES

*T*he Lord is with us! With us his creatures, the objects of his love, the work of his hands. At the summit of creation is man, made in the likeness of God and destined, as God's masterpiece, to give a name and a meaning to all creatures. But, since man turned faithless and defaced the image impressed on him by the Almighty, God chose to re-create him in another and more perfect way, through Redemption: "God with us" a second time.

DAILY PAPAL MESSAGES

$\mathcal{H}$OLINESS

You must be constantly on your guard
against pessimism.
A humble and cheerful nature,
without moods and fancies, is a great boon,
a source of success in our own lives,
and a help to others!

LETTER TO HIS NEPHEW BATTISTA,
FEBRUARY 24, 1950

*P*ractical experience has now convinced me of this: the concept of holiness which I had formed and applied to myself was mistaken. In every one of my actions, and in the little failings of which I was immediately aware, I used to call to mind the image of some saint whom I had set myself to imitate down to the smallest particular, as a painter makes an exact copy of a picture by Raphael. I used to say to myself: in this case Saint Aloysius would have done so and so, or: he would not do this or that. However, it turned out that I was never able to achieve what I had thought I could do, and this worried me. The method was wrong. From the saints I must take the substance, not the accidents, of their virtues. I am not Saint Aloysius, nor must I seek holiness in his particular way, but according to the requirements of my own nature, my own character, and the different conditions of my life. I must not be the dry, bloodless reproduction of a model, however perfect. God desires us to follow the examples of the saints by absorbing the vital sap of their virtues and turning it into our own lifeblood, adapting it to our own individual capacities and particular circumstances. If Saint Aloysius had been as I am, he would have become holy in a different way.

JOURNAL OF A SOUL, JANUARY 16, 1903

$\mathcal{W}$e are all called to be saints.

Every one of us has heard, and still hears, ringing in his conscience, the command: "Climb higher"; higher, ever higher, until while we are still on this earth we can reach up to grasp the heavens, until we can join our saints, whether they be the venerable saints of old or the wonderful saints of modern times, who were our own contemporaries, and in whom our Mother the Church already rejoices.

WRITINGS AND ADDRESSES
WHILE PATRIARCH OF VENICE

$\mathcal{L}$et all you do be natural and spontaneous, without any affectation, and look always to our Lord Jesus who reads your heart and wants you just as you are.

LETTER TO HIS NIECE GIUSEPPINA, MAY 20, 1946

$\mathcal{I}$f you should already have given way to former weaknesses, take comfort in the thought of our Lord who forgives you all, and start again from the beginning.

LETTER TO HIS FAMILY, 1901

No one can help feeling the fascination of a soul that knows what it wants, and lives by faith.

DAILY PAPAL MESSAGES

Sometimes even the desire to do well, to do better, and to love the Lord wholeheartedly produces a kind of spiritual unrest, a sense of disquiet which makes us dissatisfied with ourselves. We can never be fully satisfied with ourselves, but when this discontent saddens us and undermines our confidence, then we are falling into error or exaggeration. When this happens we must pause, recollect ourselves in silence, and then go on our way once more calmly and cheerfully. The same thing happens when we are surprised by distractions. We must go back again to the point we left in our prayer or other activity, meditation, examination of conscience, or even some external occupation, and never tire of beginning again. And we must not be overscrupulous when the intention is right and our love for the Lord is sincere.

LETTER TO HIS NIECE GIUSEPPINA,
FEBRUARY 24, 1947

Prayer is the raising of the mind to God. We must always remember this. The actual words matter less.

LETTER TO HIS NIECE GIUSEPPINA,
OCTOBER 3, 1948

Don't tire yourself with long prayers. You need only say one, the most beautiful ever uttered by human lips: *Behold the handmaid of the Lord: be it done unto me according to thy word.*

LETTER TO HIS SISTER ANCILLA,
JANUARY 11, 1953

If a life consecrated to God is to correspond better with the desire of the divine Heart, it must really be: 1) a life of prayer; 2) a life of example; 3) a life of apostolate.

LETTER TO ALL WOMEN IN RELIGIOUS LIFE

*A*s our years increase we become accustomed to the thought that we are only *lent* to this world, and so, without losing our joy in life and our wish to serve our neighbor, we find that in the depths of our hearts we are enjoying the love of Jesus which gives us life and makes us holy.

LETTER TO HIS NIECE GIUSEPPINA,
JANUARY 17, 1954

I must remember that it is my duty not only to shun evil but also to do good.

JOURNAL OF A SOUL, AUGUST 18, 1898

*M*an is made up of body and soul. The body is subjected to the most humiliating temptations: the will, which is weaker, may easily be overcome. In this mystery [of Christ's scourging] then there is a call to practice penance, a salutary penance, since it is important for man's true health, which is health in the bodily sense and also health in the sense of spiritual salvation.

There is a great lesson here for us all. We may not be called to endure a cruel martyrdom, but we are called to the exercise of constant discipline and the daily mortification of our passions. This way, a real "Way of the Cross," our daily, unavoidable, and indispensable duty, which at times becomes even heroic in its requirements, leads us step by step toward a more and more perfect resemblance with Jesus Christ, and a share in his merits and in the atonement through his innocent blood for every sin in us and in all people. We cannot do this in any other way, by facile enthusiasms, or by a fanaticism which, even if innocent, is always harmful.

SEQUENCE OF DEVOUT CONSIDERATIONS ARRANGED
FOR EACH DECADE OF THE ROSARY

The common saying, expressed in various ways and attributed to various authors, must be recalled with approval: in essentials, unity; in doubtful matters, liberty; in all things, charity.

AD PETRI CATHEDRAM

Motives for melancholy are never in short supply—and when were they ever lacking in the history of the world?—because of the inexorable alternation in human life of sadness and joy. Sometimes these mix and merge together, and when that happens we would try in vain to separate them.

A wise man, a wise Christian, must do all he can to free himself from sad thoughts, and at all times have recourse to those of comfort which transform suffering into motives of love, of merit, of present and eternal joy.

WRITINGS AND ADDRESSES
WHILE PATRIARCH OF VENICE

We must bear all cheerfully. Our life, especially that part of it which we spend in the company of others, must not be sad and gloomy; we must not let our own boredom, restlessness, and melancholy depress those who are near to us and depend on us.

In life we have to lift ourselves ever higher. There are various kinds of poetry: but the supreme poetry of this life is found in a joyful soul.

DAILY PAPAL MESSAGES

$\mathcal{E}$veryone must act according to the promptings of grace and his own personal calling, but all must share the same firm resolve to bear witness to the Divine Founder of Christianity, and this is essentially the life of God in men, and men's expectation of the life of heaven.

DAILY PAPAL MESSAGES

$\mathcal{O}$nly the man who has faith and is inspired by charity can rise above the miseries, the meannesses, and the malice of this world; instead, the man who lets himself be overcome by the spirit of illicit gain, of overweening hatred, and of impurity, is doomed to suffer, first here below, because he can never be entirely satisfied, and later on in the other world.

DAILY PAPAL MESSAGES

Nothing is more excellent than goodness. The human mind may look for other eminent gifts, but none of these can be compared with goodness. It is of the same nature as the Son of God himself, who became man, and it is the essence of all he taught us by word and example: the exercise of brotherly love and of patience, constancy in compassion and forbearance, in the interior discipline of our own characters and in the relationships of social life, just as he told us.

Jesus did not say to us: Learn from me for I am the Son of the heavenly Father. He did not show us how to create heaven and earth, or to clothe the sun in its mantle of splendor, but how to be meek and lowly of heart. This is the very foundation of goodness. When we understand the secret of goodness and have made it our own we shall have found the surest way of overcoming the difficulties and failures of our earthly life.

DAILY PAPAL MESSAGES

$\mathcal{W}$e are, alas, living in a world full of temptations and deceitful flattery. According to the ideals of this world all our activity should be directed to the search for amusements, wealth, and the enjoyment of success in all the various activities of earthly life.

When people pursue only this narrow and ephemeral aim they keep their gaze fixed on this earth and never lift their eyes to heaven. But when they live by faith, when every morning, at the first notes of the Angelus bell, they lift their minds to God and ask for his Mother's assistance, and then, through all the events of the day, encouraged by that help and those inspirations, do the duties of their work and proper state obediently, conscientiously, and faithfully, then indeed can they be truly said to have understood the real meaning of life.

By thus endowing every human act with immense significance, and living under the influence of the Holy Spirit, even their sighs and groans are able to make their own meaningful contribution to their future abundant rewards.

DAILY PAPAL MESSAGES

$\mathcal{E}$very one of us is called by the Lord: the important thing is to know how to answer his call. We must learn how to devote ourselves to Jesus, to learn from him and follow him as closely as we can, in his teaching and example; we must learn to rejoice in his company, like the disciples of Emmaus on the day of his Resurrection, like Mary and Joseph at the dawn of that life of miracles and saving grace.

DAILY PAPAL MESSAGES

$\mathcal{W}$e all like to judge events from the vantage point of the handful of earth beneath our feet. This is a great illusion. We must take our view from the heights and courageously embrace the whole.

WIT AND WISDOM OF GOOD POPE JOHN

$\mathcal{I}$t is an indisputable truth that all of us one day will receive a visit from our Sister Death, as Saint Francis of Assisi called her. She sometimes presents herself in a sudden and unexpected manner. But we shall remain tranquil, or better undisturbed, if our tree has known how to yield its fruits. He who has worked well, departs when the day has ended.

GENERAL AUDIENCE, MARCH 7, 1961

$\mathcal{P}$ut your hope and trust in those joys of heaven which Jesus has promised us. Your life, my children, is directed toward the future. I beg you: do not waste time blaming the present, or sighing for the past, which has no interest for you except insofar as it may offer you useful lessons and warnings not to repeat those mistakes which were and still are fatal for men and for nations.

ADDRESS, MAY 12, 1946

THE CHRISTIAN LIFE

The Christian faithful,
members of a living organism,
cannot remain aloof and think that they have
done their duty when they have satisfied
their own spiritual needs;
every individual must give his assistance to
those who are working for the increase
and propagation of God's kingdom.

PRINCEPS PASTORUM

*T*he sublimity of the Christian calling should shine in all its splendor before the eyes of those who embrace the Catholic religion, so that their hearts will be fired with the desire, the strong resolution to lead a life adorned with all the Christian virtues and distinguished by apostolic activity: a life, we say, modeled on the luminous example of Jesus Christ, who, taking upon himself our nature, commanded us to follow in his footsteps.

PRINCEPS PASTORUM

*T*rue Christians cannot help feeling obliged to improve their own temporal institutions and environment. They do all they can to prevent these institutions from doing violence to human dignity. They encourage whatever is conducive to honesty and virtue, and strive to eliminate every obstacle to the attainment of this aim.

MATER ET MAGISTRA

The sheer number of Christians means little if they lack virtue; that is, if, while enjoying the name of Catholic, they do not stand firm in their determination; if their spiritual life does not flourish and fails to produce wholesome fruits; if, after being reborn to divine grace, they do not excel in that spirit of vigorous and sensible youthfulness which is always ready to perform generous and useful deeds. Their profession of faith must not only be a statistic in a census, but must create a new man, and give all his actions a supernatural strength, inspiring, guiding, and controlling them.

PRINCEPS PASTORUM

Our mortal life is to be ordered in such a way as to fulfill our duties as citizens of earth and of heaven, and thus to attain the aim of life as established by God. That is, all men, whether taken singly or as united in society, today have the duty of tending ceaselessly during their lifetime toward the attainment of heavenly things and to use for this purpose only, the earthly goods, the employment of which must not prejudice their eternal happiness.

ADDRESS TO OPEN THE COUNCIL, OCTOBER 11, 1962

$\mathcal{D}$o not let yourselves be influenced by the mentality of this world which finds no peace because it has forgotten how to pray: but learn to perfume all your actions with the life-giving breath of prayer. In this way, we are sure, your life will be full of harmony and peace, full of all the blessings of heaven and earth, and you will be able to pass on to other men the power of those ideals which strengthen your heart.

DAILY PAPAL MESSAGES

$\mathcal{T}$he world, in spite of appearances to the contrary, respects Christians who are willing to serve great ideals and who are firmly anchored to something which, as we say, is valid for all times and all circumstances.

DAILY PAPAL MESSAGES

Sometimes we think we can solve in all sorts of ways the ordinary problems and difficulties of our lives. We have recourse to complicated and even to difficult means, forgetting that just a little patience is required to arrange everything in perfect order and restore calm and serenity. The Christian must treat the virtue of patience with constant and loving care, until it has become a real and excellent habit, which will result in many advantages and generous rewards.

DAILY PAPAL MESSAGES

External penance includes particularly the acceptance from God in a spirit of resignation and trust of all life's sorrows and hardships and of everything that involves inconvenience and annoyance in the conscientious performance of the obligations of our daily life and work and the practice of Christian virtue. Penance of this kind is in fact inescapable. Yet it serves not only to win God's mercy and forgiveness for our sins…but also sweetens…the bitterness of this mortal life of ours with the promise of its heavenly reward.

PAENITENTIAM AGERE

*B*esides bearing in a Christian spirit the inescapable annoyances and sufferings of this life, the faithful ought also take the initiative in doing voluntary acts of penance and offering them to God. In this they will be following in the footsteps of our divine Redeemer.

<small>PAENITENTIAM AGERE</small>

*J*esus Christ taught us self-discipline and *self-denial* when he said: "If anyone wishes to come after me, let him deny himself and take up his cross daily and follow me" [Luke 9:23]. Yet there are many people, alas, who join instead the immoderate quest for earthly pleasures, thus debasing and weakening the nobler powers of the human spirit. It is all the more necessary, therefore, for Christians to repudiate this unworthy way of life which gives frequent rein to the turbulent emotions of the soul and seriously endangers its eternal salvation. They must repudiate it with all the energy and courage displayed by the martyrs and those heroic men and women who have been the glory of the Church in every age of her history.

<small>PAENITENTIAM AGERE</small>

$\mathcal{T}$o possess freedom of choice, enlightened by a clear discriminatory sense of good and evil, right and wrong, justice and oppression, and not to honor ourselves by using this freedom rightly and defending it in the sight of God, who is ready to help us and to carry us forward to the final triumph, would mean great stupidity, and great unhappiness!

WRITINGS AND ADDRESSES
WHILE PATRIARCH OF VENICE

$\mathcal{W}$e are on this earth as wayfarers and pilgrims: there is a law and a destiny that controls all our steps, according to the time, place, and circumstances of our lives.

The end of our life is not here, but lies beyond the shores of the material world, stretching out to eternity; and eternity is the living substance of retribution, joyful or unhappy, according to the success or failure of our life and pilgrimage.

WRITINGS AND ADDRESSES
WHILE PATRIARCH OF VENICE

JUSTICE AND CHARITY

It is vain to seek to rebuild
the world upon justice;
without love no justice can last.

ADDRESS, MAY 12, 1946

$\mathcal{Y}$ou will never repent of having been over-generous in any way.

LETTER TO HIS BROTHER GIOVANNI,
MARCH 10, 1946

$\mathcal{T}$o be content with what little we have, to have our share of suffering and bless the Lord at all times, to do good to all, even to those who dislike us, to be patient and to love our fellows—this is the perfection and joy of life.

LETTER TO HIS BROTHER SAVERIO, EPIPHANY, 1948

$\mathcal{T}$he remuneration of work is not something that can be left to the laws of the market; nor ought it to be fixed arbitrarily. It must be determined in accordance with justice and equity; which means that workers must be paid a wage which allows them to live a truly human life and to fulfill their family obligations in a worthy manner.

MATER ET MAGISTRA

The economic prosperity of a nation is not so much its total assets in terms of wealth and property, as the equitable division and distribution of this wealth.

MATER ET MAGISTRA

Justice is to be observed not only in the distribution of wealth, but also in regard to the conditions in which men are engaged in producing this wealth. Every man has, of his very nature, a need to express himself in his work and thereby to perfect his own being.

Consequently, if the whole structure and organization of an economic system is such as to compromise human dignity, to lessen a man's sense of responsibility or rob him of any opportunity for exercising personal initiative, then such a system, we maintain, is altogether unjust—no matter how much wealth it produces, or how justly and equitably such wealth is distributed.

MATER ET MAGISTRA

$\mathcal{W}$ork, which is the immediate expression of a human personality, must always be rated higher than the possession of external goods which of their very nature are merely instrumental.

MATER ET MAGISTRA

$\mathcal{T}$he solidarity which binds all men together as members of a common family makes it impossible for wealthy nations to look with indifference upon the hunger, misery, and poverty of other nations whose citizens are unable to enjoy even elementary human rights. The nations of the world are becoming more and more dependent on one another, and therefore it will not be possible to preserve a lasting peace so long as these glaring economic and social inequalities persist.

MATER ET MAGISTRA

*J*ustice is born of divine wisdom, and consists in giving every man his due. Our first duty then is to render to God what belongs to God—to acknowledge him as Creator, Redeemer, and Source of all life. Then we must put into practice what he taught his disciples, telling them to carry this teaching of his to the ends of the world....

After our duty to God we must remember our obligation to give to Caesar what belongs to Caesar. This means that, when we have first of all paid our respectful homage to the Lord in the practice of our religion, we must give due consideration to our social relations.

We live on this earth; but we live by faith, and herein lies our strength. We are working for eternity, which is not of this world, but while we prepare for this final end we must learn how to live with dignity amid the trials of this present life, always subordinating all other things to what the Lord offers us in the future life. And our hope of arriving safely in eternity rests very largely on our constant respect for the rights of our fellow men.

DAILY PAPAL MESSAGES

All work becomes supremely great when it is done in the spirit of our Lord.

Daily Papal Messages

There is no learning or wealth, there is no human power that is more effective than a good nature, a heart that is gentle, friendly, and patient. The good-hearted man may suffer mortifications and opposition, but he always wins through in the end because his goodness is love, and love is all-conquering.

All through life, and especially at its end, the happiest tribute of praise is always the same: "he was so good, he had such a kind heart." And his name brings joy and blessing.

It is a mistake to think that kindness, that is, true friendliness, is but a minor virtue. It is a great virtue because it means self-control and a disinterested intention, with a fervent love of justice. It is the expression and the splendor of brotherly love, in the grace of Jesus. It is the way to attain human and divine perfection.

Writings and Addresses
while Patriarch of Venice

$\mathcal{L}$et men make all the technical and economic progress they can, there will be no peace nor justice in the world until they return to a sense of their dignity as creatures and sons of God, who is the first and final cause of all created Being. Separated from God, a man is but a monster, in himself and toward others; for the right ordering of human society presupposes the right ordering of man's conscience with God, who is himself the source of all justice, truth, and love.

MATER ET MAGISTRA

PEACE

There can be no peace between men
unless there is peace within each one of them,
unless, that is, each one builds up
within himself the order wished by God.

PACEM IN TERRIS

The dead encourage us to sanctify the years or days that still remain for us to live: let us try to live in peace and charity with those who are still alive, doing good to all to the extent of our power.

LETTER TO HIS COUSIN MARIA, JULY 14, 1937

War is the ruin of civilization and the return to barbarism. Even if the need to resist violence with force, the defense of security or of essential liberty, makes it seem inevitable, war must always be the last resource.

LETTER TO FRENCH PRESIDENT VINCENT AURIOL, DECEMBER 30, 1950

True peace is born of doing the will of God, and bearing with patience the sufferings of this life, and does not come from following one's own whim or selfish desire, for this always brings, not peace and serenity, but disorder and discontent.

DAILY PAPAL MESSAGES

$\mathcal{N}$o peace will have solid foundations unless hearts nourish the sentiment of brotherhood which ought to exist among all who have a common origin and are called to the same destiny. The knowledge that they belong to the same family extinguishes lust, greed, pride, and the instinct to dominate others, which are the roots of dissensions and wars. It binds all in a single bond of higher and more fruitful solidarity.

CHRISTMAS MESSAGE, DECEMBER 23, 1959

$\mathcal{L}$ove for one's neighbor and one's own people ought not to be concentrated on one's self in an exclusive egotism which is suspicious of another's good. But it ought to expand and reach out spontaneously toward the community of interests, to embrace all peoples and to interweave common human relations. Thus it will be possible to speak of living together, and not of mere coexistence which, precisely because it is deprived of this inspiration of mutual dependence, raises barriers behind which nestle mutual suspicion, fear, and terror.

CHRISTMAS MESSAGE, DECEMBER 23, 1959

$\mathcal{M}$ay no one assume to himself the right of destroying human lives! May all see, instead, in every man the image of God the Creator, Father of us all, and may the hands of those who are brothers in Christ the Redeemer be joined together.

ADDRESS, JUNE 3, 1962

$\mathcal{M}$ay all our children, may all those who have been marked with the seal of baptism and nourished by Christian hope, may all those, finally, who are united to us by faith in God, join their prayers to ours to obtain from heaven the gift of peace: a peace which will be true and lasting only if it is based on justice and equity.

And upon all those who contribute to this peace, upon all those who work with a sincere heart for the true welfare of men, may there descend the special blessing which we lovingly bestow in the name of him who wished to be called the "Prince of Peace."

BROADCAST TO WORLD LEADERS, OCTOBER 25, 1962

$\mathscr{A}$ll must realize that there is no hope of putting an end to the building up of armaments, nor of reducing the present stocks, nor, still less—and this is the main point—of abolishing them altogether, unless the process is complete and thorough and unless it proceeds from inner conviction: unless, that is, everyone sincerely cooperates to banish the fear and anxious expectation of war with which men are oppressed. If this is to come about, the fundamental principle on which our present peace depends must be replaced by another, which declares that the true and solid peace of nations consists not in equality of arms but in mutual trust alone. We believe that this can be brought to pass, and we consider that, since it concerns a matter not only demanded by right reason but also eminently desirable in itself, it will prove to be the source of many benefits.

Pacem in Terris

$\mathscr{U}$nless peace, unity, and concord are present in domestic society, how can they exist in civil society?

Ad Petri Cathedram

$\mathscr{A}$mong all the good things of our lives and of our history, enjoyed by individuals, families, and peoples, peace is truly the most important and the most precious. The presence of peace, and the endeavor to achieve it, are the guarantee of tranquillity in this world. But peace is conditioned by the goodwill of one and all, peace to men of goodwill, because wherever this goodwill is lacking it is useless to hope for joy and blessings.

So we must seek peace at all times: we must try to create it in our own circle, so that it may spread throughout the world, and we must defend it from all dangers and in all trials, making sure never to offend or compromise it.

DAILY PAPAL MESSAGES

$\mathscr{P}$eace will be but an empty-sounding word unless it is...founded on truth, built according to justice, vivified and integrated by charity, and put into practice in freedom.

PACEM IN TERRIS

TRUTH

Where Christ has been left out,
ignorance abounds.

DAILY PAPAL MESSAGES

$\mathcal{A}$ll the evils which poison men and nations and trouble so many hearts have a single cause and a single source: ignorance of the truth—and at times even more than ignorance, a contempt for truth and a reckless rejection of it. Thus arise all manner of errors, which enter the recesses of men's hearts and the bloodstream of human society as would a plague. These errors turn everything upside down: they menace individuals and society itself.

And yet, God gave each of us an intellect capable of attaining natural truth. If we adhere to this truth, we adhere to God himself, the author of truth, the lawgiver and ruler of our lives. But if we reject this truth, whether out of foolishness, neglect, or malice, we turn our backs on the highest good itself and on the very norm for right living.

AD PETRI CATHEDRAM

The child's mother teaches him to have a horror of falsehood; as the years go by the grown man clearly perceives that truth is always our salvation, that compromise with the truth must at all times be rejected, and that in social relations a man's honor is judged by his fidelity, at all times, to the truth.

DAILY PAPAL MESSAGES

Anyone who deems himself a Christian must know that he is bound by his conscience to the basic, imperative duty of bearing witness to the truth in which he believes and to the grace which has transformed his soul.

PRINCEPS PASTORUM

Only the truth of Christ can make us free (cf. John 8:32); it gives the answer which everyone awaits but which at times—because of the great effort it demands—everyone is afraid to hear. Be then living witnesses of the truth, and by so doing your hearts will always be full of sincere and profound joy.

DAILY PAPAL MESSAGES

One must never confuse error and the person who errs, not even when there is question of error or inadequate knowledge of truth in the moral or religious field. The person who errs is always and above all a human being, and he retains in every case his dignity as a human person; and he must be always regarded and treated in accordance with that lofty dignity. Besides, in every human being, there is a need that is congenital to this nature and never becomes extinguished, compelling him to break through the web of error and open his mind to the knowledge of truth. And God will never fail to act on his interior being, with the result that a person, who at a given moment of his life lacked the clarity of faith or even adheres to erroneous doctrines, can at a future date be enlightened and believe the truth.

PACEM IN TERRIS

To expect everything here below from this world alone, this poor world which is merely a passageway, or a place of trial, is an illusion. For here we have no lasting city for our sojourn, and we must look for our true fatherland that is to come.

One of the commonest illusions is that we can settle down here below as if we were permanent landlords of the tiny plot of ground on which we stand, living and behaving as if we were the owners and not simply the custodians of what is provided for the common good of all men, according to the laws of divine and human justice.

WRITINGS AND ADDRESSES
WHILE PATRIARCH OF VENICE

It is natural that the souls created by God and destined for eternal life should seek to discover the truth, the primary object of the human mind's activity. Why must we speak the truth? Because truth comes from God, and between man and the truth there is no merely accidental relationship but one which is necessary and essential.

DAILY PAPAL MESSAGES

*W*hat a magnificent program this is for Christian life and for apostolic social activity! To live in Christ who is divine light, universal charity; to move in his footsteps and his company: *in ipso manere: cum ipso ambulare,* which means an activity that is dynamic yet calm, orderly, and peaceful, in praise of God, and in the service of justice, of fairness, of brotherhood as Christians and human beings.

If we act in this way and move in this direction, then we are in the truth—let us say it humbly in the words of our Saint John—we are in the Truth, that is to say, in God: in his Son Jesus Christ, to whom be glory and benediction through all ages. Amen, Amen.

ADDRESS, MAY 14, 1961

*T*here is one truth especially which we think is self-evident: when the sacred rights of God and religion are ignored or infringed upon, the foundations of human society will sooner or later crumble and give way.

AD PETRI CATHEDRAM

ℳODERN ISSUES

*The lone voice is not likely
to command much of a hearing
in times such as ours.*

MATER ET MAGISTRA

It has been claimed that in an era of scientific and technical triumphs such as ours man can well afford to rely on his own powers, and construct a very good civilization without God. But the truth is that these very advances in science and technology frequently involve the whole human race in such difficulties as can only be solved in the light of a sincere faith in God, the Creator and Ruler of man and his world.

MATER ET MAGISTRA

The most fundamental modern error is that of imagining that man's natural sense of religion is nothing more than the outcome of feeling or fantasy, to be eradicated from his soul as an anachronism and an obstacle to human progress. And yet this very need for religion reveals a man for what he is: a being created by God and tending always toward God.

MATER ET MAGISTRA

$\mathcal{I}$t is necessary that human beings, in the intimacy of their own consciences, should so live and act in their temporal lives as to create a synthesis between scientific, technical, and professional elements on the one hand, and spiritual values on the other.

PACEM IN TERRIS

$\mathcal{T}$he moral order has no existence except in God; cut off from God it must necessarily disintegrate. Moreover, man is not just a material organism. He consists also of spirit; he is endowed with thought and freedom. He demands, therefore, a moral and religious order; and it is this order—and not considerations of a purely extraneous, material order—which has the greatest validity in the solution of problems relating to his life as an individual and as a member of society, and problems concerning individual states and their interrelations.

MATER ET MAGISTRA

*O*n the Lord's Day the faithful must stop being men of machines and worldly business; they must really abstain from work, not only from what is called "servile" work, but from other labors also, because they rob the mind of its rest, which it needs in order to be able to rise to heavenly things in prayer, to take an active share in the liturgical life of the Church, and to meditate upon the Word of God.

DAILY PAPAL MESSAGES

*S*uch, in every age, is the task of the human intelligence: to garner the wisdom of the ages, to hand down the good doctrine and firmly and humbly to press ahead with scientific investigation. We die, one after the other, we go to God, but mankind moves toward the future.

SEQUENCE OF DEVOUT CONSIDERATIONS
ARRANGED FOR EACH DECADE OF THE ROSARY

So much toil and effort is expended today in mastering and advancing human knowledge that our age glories—and rightly—in the amazing progress it has made in the field of scientific research. But why do we not devote as much energy, ingenuity, and enthusiasm to the sure and safe attainment of that learning which concerns not this earthly, mortal life but the life which lies ahead of us in heaven? Our spirit will rest in peace and joy only when we have reached that truth which is taught in the gospels and which should be reduced to action in our lives. This is a joy which surpasses by far any pleasure which can come from the study of things human or from those marvelous inventions which we use today and are constantly praising to the skies.

AD PETRI CATHEDRAM

Private ownership of property is a natural right which the State cannot suppress. It includes the ownership of productive goods, but naturally brings with it also an intrinsic obligation to society. It is a right which must be exercised not only for one's own personal benefit but also for the benefit of others.

MATER ET MAGISTRA

$\mathscr{I}$n a system of taxation based on justice
and equity…the burdens [must] be
proportioned to the capacity of the people
contributing.

M ATER ET M AGISTRA

$\mathscr{I}$t is not possible to determine "a priori"
what the structure of farm life should be, since
rural conditions vary so much from place to
place and from country to country throughout
the world. But if we hold to a human and
Christian concept of man and the family, we
are bound to consider as an ideal that form of
enterprise which is modeled on the basis of a
community of persons working together for the
advancement of their mutual interests in
accordance with the principles of justice and
Christian teaching. We are bound above all to
consider as an ideal the kind of farm which is
owned and managed by the family. Every effort
must be made in the prevailing circumstances
to give effective encouragement to farming
enterprises of this nature.

M ATER ET M AGISTRA

$\mathcal{J}$ustice and humanity demand that those countries which produce consumer goods, especially farm products, in excess of their own needs should come to the assistance of those other countries where large sections of the population are suffering from want and hunger. It is nothing less than an outrage to justice and humanity to destroy or to squander goods that other people need for their very lives.

We are, of course, well aware that overproduction, especially in agriculture, can cause economic harm to a certain section of the population. But it does not follow that one is thereby exonerated from extending emergency aid to those who need it. On the contrary, everything must be done to minimize the ill effects of overproduction, and to spread the burden equitably over the entire population.

MATER ET MAGISTRA

Human life is transmitted by means of the family, and the family is based upon a marriage which is one and indissoluble and raised, so far as Christians are concerned, to the dignity of a sacrament. The transmission of human life is the result of a personal and conscious act, and, as such, is subject to the all-holy, inviolable, and immutable laws of God, which a man ignores and disobeys to his cost. He is not therefore permitted to use certain ways and means which are allowable in the propagation of plant and animal life.

Human life is sacred—all men must recognize that fact. From its very inception it betrays the creating hand of God. Those who violate his laws not only offend the divine Majesty and degrade themselves and humanity, they also sap the vitality of the State of which they are members.

MATER ET MAGISTRA

To proceed gradually is the law of life in all its expressions; therefore in human institutions, too, it is not possible to renovate for the better except by working from within them, gradually.

PACEM IN TERRIS

We exhort our children to take an active part in public life, and to contribute toward the attainment of the common good of the entire human family as well as to that of their own country. They should endeavor, therefore, in the light of the Faith and with the strength of love, to ensure that the various institutions—whether economic, social, cultural, or political in purpose—should be such as not to create obstacles, but rather to facilitate or render less arduous man's perfecting of himself both in the natural order as well as in the supernatural.

PACEM IN TERRIS

Individual human beings are the foundation, the cause, and the end of every social institution. That is necessarily so, for men are by nature social beings. This fact must be recognized, as also the fact that they are raised in the plan of Providence to an order of reality which is above nature.

On this basic principle, which guarantees the sacred dignity of the individual, the Church constructs the whole of her social teaching.

MATER ET MAGISTRA

THE CHURCH AND THE SACRAMENTS

*The Catholic Church is not an
archaeological museum.
It is the ancient village fountain that gives
water to the generations of today,
as it gave it to those of days gone by.*

ADDRESS AFTER MASS, NOVEMBER 13, 1960

O Holy Church of God, in vain men ignored you, in vain they excluded you from the affairs of human society: you are here, as you will always be, always recognizable, always suffering maybe, but always queen! Your opposition to the principles and prejudices of the world sometimes engages you in difficult situations and in long periods of reverses, even of humiliations, which here and there might look like defeats—but you will never die.

SERMON, JUNE 24, 1945

*E*ven though the main goal toward which the Church is striving is not an earthly one, still, as she journeys along her path, she cannot ignore the questions that have to do with temporal goods or pay no attention to the labors that produce these goods. She is well aware of the precise benefit that can be conferred on immortal souls by whatever serves to make a little more human the lives of individual men, whose eternal salvation she is seeking. She realizes that when she sheds the light of Christ upon men, she is helping them to know themselves better. For she leads them to understand what they really are, what dignity they enjoy, what goal they must pursue.

HUMANAE SALUTIS

*W*hat a joy it is to belong to Holy Church! It is one large family of saints, saints on earth who are related to saints in heaven. The world understands nothing of all this.

LETTER TO HIS NEPHEW BATTISTA,
FEBRUARY 20, 1946

*T*o share in our brothers' pain, to suffer with those who suffer, to weep with those who weep, will confer a blessing, a merit on the whole Church. Is this not what we mean by the "communion of saints," every one of us sharing in common the blood of Jesus, the love of the saints and of good people, and also, alas! our sins and failings? Do we ever think of this "communion" which is union, and almost, as Jesus said, unity: "That they may be one"? The Lord's Cross not only raises us up but draws the souls of men, always: "And I, when I am lifted up, will draw all men to myself." All things, all men.

SEQUENCE OF DEVOUT CONSIDERATIONS
ARRANGED FOR EACH DECADE OF THE ROSARY

This is the mission of the Church, catholic and apostolic, to reunite men whom selfishness and disillusionment might keep apart, to show them how to pray, to bring them to contrition for their sins and to forgiveness, to feed them with the Eucharistic Bread, and to bind them together with the bonds of charity.

DAILY PAPAL MESSAGES

The Church…does not identify itself with any one culture, not even with European and Western civilization, although the history of the Church is closely intertwined with it; for the mission entrusted to the Church pertains chiefly to other matters, that is, to matters which are concerned with religion and the eternal salvation of men. The Church, however, which is so full of youthful vigor and is constantly renewed by the breath of the Holy Spirit, is willing, at all times, to recognize, welcome, and even assimilate anything that redounds to the honor of the human mind and heart.

PRINCEPS PASTORUM

In the Church of Christ, if love is queen, no prince of darkness can prevail.

AETERNA DEI SAPIENTIA

Sometimes Christ is like an arrow: an arrow that wounds a little bird, that continues to fly although this tiny wound will cause its death. And our action will be like a little wound, a tiny thing which has pierced a soul, and through this little wound something of Christ has entered; the soul has been as it were pierced and dies of this wound, but the result is not death but life.

At times we seem to be engaged in hunting souls in this way and when evening comes and we go over the different actions of the day to count our successes, we feel we have wasted our time and we are tempted to set our bow and arrow aside.

And yet we have had some success, for sometimes, years afterward, we find that our arrow had reached and wounded a soul.

ADDRESS, MARCH 15, 1945

The Catholic Church is set apart and distinguished by these three characteristics: unity of doctrine, unity of organization, unity of worship. This unity is so conspicuous that by it all men can find and recognize the Catholic Church.

AD PETRI CATHEDRAM

When I confess, I must beg Jesus first of all to be my wisdom, helping me to make a calm, precise, detailed examination of my sins and of their gravity, so that I may feel sincere sorrow for them. Then, that he may be my justice, so that I may present myself to my confessor as to my judge and accuse myself sincerely and sorrowfully. May he be also my perfect sanctification when I bow my head to receive absolution from the hand of the priest, by whose gesture is restored or increased sanctifying grace. Finally, that he may be my redemption as I perform that meager penance which is set me instead of the great penalty I deserve: a meager penance indeed, but a rich atonement because it is united with the sacrament to the blood of Christ, which intercedes and atones and washes and cleanses, for me and with me.

JOURNAL OF A SOUL, NOVEMBER 26, 1940

$\mathcal{D}$oing penance for one's sins is a first step toward obtaining forgiveness and winning eternal salvation....No individual Christian can grow in perfection, nor can Christianity itself gain in vigor, except it be on this basis of penance.

PAENITENTIAM AGERE

$\mathcal{O}$ur first need is for internal repentance; the detestation, that is, of sin, and the determination to make amends for it. This is the repentance shown by those who make a good confession, take part in the Eucharistic Sacrifice, and receive Holy Communion.

PAENITENTIAM AGERE

The Mass is a poem, divided into various parts. But, in spite of our good intentions, our imagination often strays and distracts us. This does not matter. We become recollected once more, ashamed of our weaknesses, and inspired with new fervor. Then in some mysterious way the distraction and the recollection together form one single sacrifice which the Lord accepts "in the odor of sweetness."

LETTER TO HIS NEPHEW BATTISTA,
JANUARY 16, 1947

The Mass is the adorable sacrifice in which God himself is at the same time Victim, Priest, and the divine Majesty to whom the sacrifice is offered; not merely the symbol of the sacrifice of the Cross but the sacrifice itself, mysteriously renewed and reenacted for ever, without the shedding of blood.

It is an infinite sacrifice, the efficacy of which is restricted only by our own lack of fervor and devotion.

All light in this world streams from the Sacrifice of the Mass. There is no alleviation of the pains of purgatory that is not distilled like balm from the overflowing chalice of the Eucharist; there is no increase of heavenly glory but through this Sacrifice. Moreover, and this is a much graver thing: no newcomer can enter heaven except through the Sacrifice ever present in the Mass.

It is impossible to find or imagine a closer bond between Man and God.

WRITINGS AND ADDRESSES
WHILE PATRIARCH OF VENICE

*T*he Name, the Heart, the Blood of Jesus: here you have the substantial nourishment for a solid life of piety.

LETTER TO ALL WOMEN IN RELIGIOUS LIFE

A Christian formation and education which would only consider teaching the faithful the formulas of the catechism and inculcating in their minds the principal precepts of moral theology, with a brief list of possible cases, without inspiring their souls and wills to act according to the instructions received, would run the serious risk of acquiring for the Church a passive flock.

PRINCEPS PASTORUM

The great problem confronting the world after almost two thousand years remains unchanged. Christ is ever resplendent as the center of history and of life. Men are either with him and his Church, and then they enjoy light, goodness, order, and peace. Or else they are without him, or against him, and deliberately opposed to his Church, and then they give rise to confusion, to bitterness in human relations, and to the constant danger of fratricidal wars.

ADDRESS TO OPEN THE COUNCIL, OCTOBER 11, 1962

Holy mother Church is always alive and flourishing with perpetual youth, always involved in human events, and always, in the course of the centuries, adorned with a fresh appearance, radiating new glories, bearing new palms, even while remaining always the same perfect picture of that form which her divine Spouse, who loves and protects her, we mean Christ Jesus, willed her to have.

HUMANAE SALUTIS

$\mathcal{I}$n the present order of things, Divine Providence is leading us to a new order of human relations which, by men's own efforts and even beyond their very expectations, are directed toward the fulfillment of God's superior and inscrutable designs. And everything, even human differences, leads to the greater good of the Church.

ADDRESS TO OPEN THE COUNCIL, OCTOBER 11, 1962

$\mathcal{T}$he Church has the right and obligation not merely to guard ethical and religious principles, but also to declare its authoritative judgment in the matter of putting these principles into practice.

MATER ET MAGISTRA

$\mathcal{L}$et us pray with one another and for one another, and for all the scattered creatures of God who make up the Holy Church and the human family, which is also all his own.

RADIO ADDRESS, SEPTEMBER 10, 1961

VATICAN II

*I abide by the sound doctrine which
teaches that everything comes from God.
In this very sense I have considered
as a heavenly inspiration
the idea for the Council. . . .*

ADDRESS TO NON-CATHOLICS AT THE COUNCIL,
OCTOBER 13, 1962

$\mathcal{B}$y God's grace may this Second Vatican Council…arouse such a potential of spiritual energy in the Church, may it so extend the field of the Catholic apostolate, that men everywhere, led by the Spouse of Christ, may attain their loftiest and most ambitious aims, which till now have eluded their grasp.

A magnificent hope indeed! It concerns not only the Church, but the whole brotherhood of men.

LETTER TO THE FATHERS OF THE COUNCIL,
JANUARY 6, 1963

$\mathcal{W}$e have had in our mind's eye this twofold picture: on the one hand, human society laboring under a great need for spiritual goods; on the other, the Church of Christ flourishing with a fullness of life. This picture has been before our eyes since the very beginning of our supreme pontificate, to whose heights we were raised despite our unworthiness by the most gracious plan of God in his providence.

As we gazed upon this picture, we considered it a serious responsibility of our apostolic office to direct our thoughts toward having the Church, through the cooperation of all our sons, show herself better and better fitted to solve the problems of the men of this age. For this reason, and in response to an inner voice that arose from a kind of heavenly inspiration, we felt that the time was ripe for us to give the Catholic Church and the whole human family the gift of a new ecumenical council, which would continue that series of twenty synods which have been of such great value for the growth of heavenly grace in the souls of the faithful and for the progress of Christianity in the course of the centuries.

HUMANAE SALUTIS

$\mathcal{B}$ishops from every part of the world will gather…to discuss serious religious topics. They will consider, in particular, the growth of the Catholic faith, the restoration of sound morals among the Christian flock, and appropriate adaptation of Church discipline to the needs and conditions of our times.

This event will be a wonderful spectacle of truth, unity, and charity. For those who behold it but are not one with this Apostolic See, we hope that it will be a gentle invitation to seek and find that unity for which Jesus Christ prayed so ardently to his Father in heaven.

AD PETRI CATHEDRAM

$\mathcal{W}$e feel sure that the decisions made in the ecumenical synod will have the effect not only of shedding the light of Christian wisdom and supplying strength and ardor to the hearts and minds of individuals but also of permeating the whole range of human activities.

Humanae Salutis

$\mathcal{W}$e ask each of the faithful and the Christian people as a whole to devote every effort to the Council and to pour forth great prayers to Almighty God graciously to sustain this great undertaking…and to strengthen it with his virtue and power….May these common prayers flow steadily from faith as from a living font; may they be accompanied by voluntary bodily mortification to make them more acceptable to God and supremely effective; may they also be enriched by an unselfish effort to live a Christian life, which would be a sign that all are already prepared to carry out the precepts and decrees…laid down by this council.

Humanae Salutis

The Council now beginning rises in the Church like daybreak, a forerunner of most splendid light. It is now only dawn. And already at this first announcement of the rising day, how much sweetness fills our heart.

ADDRESS TO OPEN THE COUNCIL, OCTOBER 11, 1962

The outcome of the approaching ecumenical council will depend more on a crusade of fervent prayer than on human effort and diligent application.

AD PETRI CATHEDRAM

May the Holy Family protect all our

own homes and those of our relatives,

and the whole Christian family

scattered throughout the world.

May they protect and bless us as

I now bless you.

———

LETTER TO HIS FAMILY, JULY 30, 1944

$\mathcal{P}$ERMISSIONS AND ACKNOWLEDGMENTS

Every effort has been made to locate and secure permission for the inclusion of all copyrighted material in this book. If any such acknowledgments have been inadvertently omitted, the publisher would appreciate receiving full information so that proper credit may be given in future editions.

Selections from *Ad Petri Cathedram, Aeterna Dei Sapientia, Humanae Salutis, Mater et Magistra, Pacem in Terris, Paenitentiam Agere,* and *Princeps Pastorum* are reprinted by permission of Libreria Editrice Vaticana, 00120 Città del Vaticano.

Selections from Writings and Addresses while Patriarch of Venice and Daily Papal Messages are reprinted by permission from *Days of Devotion: Daily Meditations from the Good Shepherd,* Pope John XXIII, New York: Viking Penguin, 1996, copyright 1967 The K. S. Giniger Company, Inc.

Selections from John XXIII's letters to his family are reprinted from *Letters to His Family,* Pope John XXIII, trans. Dorothy White, New York: McGraw-Hill, 1969.

Selections from John XXIII's journals are reprinted from *Journal of a Soul* (see page 1ff), Pope John XXIII, trans. Dorothy White, New York: McGraw-Hill, 1964.

Selections from John XXIII's messages and correspondence while apostolic nuncio in France are reprinted from *Mission to France* (see page 72), *1944–1953,* Angelo Giuseppe Roncalli, ed. Don Loris Capovilla, trans. Dorothy White, New York: McGraw-Hill, 1966.

Selections of John XXIII's witticisms are reprinted from *Wit and Wisdom of Good Pope John,* collected by Henri Fesquet, trans. Salvator Attanasio, P. J. Kenedy & Sons: New York, 1964.

PHOTOS
page ii: Pope John XXIII. (*CNS photo*)

page v: Pope John XXIII greets crowds from train. (*CORBIS/ Bettmann*)

page 111: Queen Elizabeth and Pope John XXIII. (*CORBIS/ Hulton-Deutsch Collection*)